Spartans

The True and Brutal Story of How the Spartans Become the Strongest Warriors in History

Table of Contents

3

Introduction

I want to thank you and congratulate you for downloading the book, *"Spartans: The True and Brutal Story of How the Spartans Become the Strongest Warriors in History"*.

"The Spartans used to ask about the enemy, it was not important how many there are, but where the enemy was" (Plutarch, *Moralia*[1]).

This book contains specific evidence of the steps and strategies on how to live, train, and fight like the Spartans on the battlefield. In addition, this book provides an in-depth examination of the daily lives of the Spartan people in terms of their rituals, gender roles, courtship traditions, as well as some of their leisure activities including javelin tosses. Not only will you be able to learn how to battle like a Spartan, but you may also learn to adopt the simplistic Spartan way of life. Finally, as you progress through the chapters of this book, you will learn the details of some of the most famous battles in Greece fought by the Spartans which led to their rise and fall in terms of authoritative power. Most interestingly is that, through reading this book, you may find some similarities between the political and social actions of the Spartans and the modern-day western views and traditions relating to government. So, strap your feet into your sandals, throw on your finest bronze armor, raise your swords to the sky, and let out your best battle cries as you begin this guided journey through the city-state of Sparta from the prehistoric and Middle Neolithic

---

[1] Plutarch, "Apophthegmata Laconica," *Moralia* trans. Frank Cole Babbit, ed. *Moralia* Vol. III Loeb Classical Library, Cambridge: Harvard University Press, 2004

periods to the classical Sparta period beginning around 480 B.C. as well as the Hellenistic and Roman Sparta periods beginning around 371 B.C. and 146 B.C.

Thanks again for downloading this book, I hope you enjoy it!

Copyright Information

Chapter 1:
The Daily Life of the Spartans

A Brief History of the Spartans

"This is Sparta!" (*300*, 2006[2]). Many have quoted this famous line of dialogue from the 2006 blockbuster hit *300*. In fact, over the years, there have been several films based on the history of Sparta. But what exactly was Sparta and who were the Spartans? Sparta was a society located the region of Laconia in ancient Greece that rose to its highest power between 431 and 401 B.C. The people who inhabited to society of Sparta—the Spartans—were a highly loyal militant group, the men receiving intense training for battle when they were only boys and the women, unlike most Greek women at the time, were trained to become intellectual members of society.

From the Prehistoric Period to the Archaic Period

Although the literary evidence regarding events during the prehistoric period of the Spartans is not completely clear, the earliest sound evidence of humans settling within the vicinity of Sparta comes from pottery dating back to the Middle Neolithic period (also known as the "New Stone Age"), found just 1.2 miles southwest of Sparta. Such artifacts are the oldest pieces of evidence of the Mycenaean Spartans, settlers during

---

[2] *300*. Dir. Zack Snyder. Warner Bros. Legendary Pictures, Virtual Studios, Hollywood Gang Productions, Atmosphere Entertainment MM, Mel's Cite du Cinema, Nimar Studios, 2006

the final phase of the Bronze Age in Greece, which were reflected in Homer's *Iliad*. By the end of the Bronze Age, the civilization began to fall due to Macedonian tribes invading Peloponnese, where they were referred to as "Dorians." The Dorians made plans to settle and start a new frontier in Spartan territory, battling the Argive Dorians east and southeast of Sparta as well as the Arcadian Archaeans northwest of Sparta. To date, there has not been any distinct archaeological evidence of the Dorians or the Dorian Spartan civilization along the Eurotas River Valley, where the city of Sparta is located.

The Dark Age of Spartan history is believed to be legendary in that it deals with the Greek mythology, including heroes such as the Heraclids and the Perseids, combining both fictional events and possible historical ones. It is this period of Sparta that provides the first believable sources of Spartan history. From an archaeological standpoint, it is presumed that the first Spartan settlement began around 1000 B.C., two hundred years after the fall of the Mycenaean civilization. It is possible that Sparta's dual kingship government originated from a combining of two Spartan villages during this time period.

Classical Sparta

The Spartans faced a stretch of anarchy and civil conflict during the 7th and 8th centuries B.C. and because of this, a number of political and social policy changes were carried out which the Spartans later linked to the mythological lawmaker, Lycurgus. These changes in Spartan society are used as a starting point for the Classical Sparta period of civilization. During the Second Messenian War, Sparta was established as a local authority in Peloponnese and the remainder of ancient Greece. In the centuries to follow, the Spartans original reputation as a land-fighting people was incomparable to other civilizations in Greece. It is during the Classical Sparta age that the Spartans took part in the famous battles of Thermopylae and the battle of Plataea.

In the latter part of Classical Sparta, Sparta along with Athens, Thebes, and Persia had been the main states battling for dominance over each other in the Peloponnesian War. As an outcome of this war, Sparta became seafaring warriors. Classical Sparta saw the threshold of Spartan power over even the most elite Athenian naval force. As Classical Sparta approached the 5th century B.C., Sparta caught the eyes of many as a society of people who defeated the Athenians overtook Persian territories in Anatolia, marking the period of Sparta's greatest military on land called the Spartan Hegemony.

In the Corinthian War that followed, Sparta was faced with an alliance of the most powerful states in ancient Greece: Thebes, Athens, Corinth, and Argos. This four-way partnership was originally supported by Persia, which had previously been invaded by Sparta in territories within Anatolia and Persians were concerned that the Spartans would expand their invasion further into Asia. Although the Spartans were victorious on land, they did not fare as well on sea as many of their battleships were obliterated during the battle of Cnidus in which Persia provided Athens with a mercenary fleet of Greek-Phoenician warriors. Due to this defeat, Sparta's naval power was severely impaired but the Spartans did not give up their ambitions of invading more territories in Persia until the Athenian general Conon tore apart the Spartan coastline and instilled fear in the Spartans of a rebellion by the helots, state-owned slaves in Sparta.

In 387 B.C., an agreement was set in place called the Peace of Antalcidas which permitted all cities within the state of Ionia in Greece would go back to being under the control of Persia and the Asian border aligning with Persia would no longer be under the control of the Spartans. The outcome of the war was to restate Persia's ability to successfully take part in Greek politics and to reiterate Sparta's declining role in Greek politics. Sparta's rapid decline began after being defeated by the Theban general Epaminondas during the battle of Leuctra, the first land battle lost by the Spartans. Because Spartan citizenship required a blood relation to the original ancestors of Sparta, the enslaved helots began to outnumber the Spartans, leading to the decline of their civilization.

Hellenistic and Roman Sparta

After the battle of Leuctra, Sparta's never completely bounced back from the decline in their citizen population and the revolt of the helots. However, Sparta continued on as a regional authority for the next two centuries. Despite their power, neither the historical icons Philip II or Alexander the Great bothered trying to take over Sparta itself. Going forward, Sparta was often known as the "defender of Hellenism" (Wikipedia[3]) and for its laconic wit even when its population was declining. In an attempt to unify the Greek states against Persian rule, Philip II concocted a league of the Greeks and the Spartans, being the rebels that they were, chose not to participate. The Spartans were not interested in the Greek

---

[3] Wikipedia "4th Century BC," *History of Sparta* 5 Mar. 2016. Web.   6   Mar.   2016 https://en.wikipedia.org/wiki/History_of_Sparta#cite_ref-97

crusade unless they were able to lead the group. Upon conquering Persia, Alexander the Great, who stood by the league of the Greeks, sent the Athenians three hundred Persian armor suits each with an inscription that read "Alexander, son of Philip, and all the Greeks except the Spartans, give these offerings taken from the foreigners who live in Asia" (Wikipedia[4]).

In 333 B.C., during Alexander the Great's reign over eastern Greece, Agis III, the Spartan king at the time, sent a troop of Spartans to Crete in order to maintain a tight grip on the island of Sparta. Then Agis III took hold of allied Greek militant groups. A large Macedonian military led by the general Antipater defeated the Spartan forces in battle, killing more than 5,300 Spartans as well as their allies compared to the 3,500 men who died in Antipater's armed forces. Agis III, who suffered from a combat-related injury, requested that his troops go on without him as he faced the approaching Macedonian military forces in order to buy his troops time to go into hiding. Agis III slayed several rival soldiers before finally being killed on the battlefield. Alexander the Great, displaying a small amount of generosity to the Spartans, only forced them to join the league of Corinth but did not push them to join the rest of the Greeks.

During the Punic Wars, a series of three distinct wars that were fought in Rome, Sparta remained in an alliance with the Roman Republic. The Spartans no longer possessed political independence when forced to join forces with the Archaean League following their loss to other Greek city-states as well as

---

[4] Wikipedia "Hellenistic and Roman Sparta," *Sparta* 29 Feb. 2016. Web. 6 Mar. 2016 https://en.wikipedia.org/wiki/Sparta

Rome in the Laconian War and the overthrow of Sparta's last king Nabis. One hundred forty-six B.C. saw Greece being taken over by the Roman general Lucius Mummius but the Spartans continued with their own policies and way of life, becoming a hot spot for Roman tourists curious to observe the unique customs in Sparta.

Medieval and Modern Sparta

Byzantine sources suggest that certain parts of the Laconian region of Greece remained pagan by nature far into the 10th century A.D. Populations speaking in a Dorian dialect still exist today in Tsakonia, a small region located in eastern Peloponnese. During the Middle Ages, the political and cultural heart of Laconia migrated to the neighboring settlement of Mystras and Sparta's significance in power declined at an even greater rate. In 1834, Sparta was founded once again by a descendant of the Greek king Otto.

Structure of Spartan Society

The Spartan society was constructed as an oligarchy, a governmental design in which power lies within the hands of a select few individuals within the state. Sparta was governed by two hereditary kings from the Agiad and Eurypontid clans, both assumed to be descendants of Heracles (commonly known as Hercules), the Greek mythological god of strength, heroes, sports, athletes, health, agriculture, fertility, trade, oracles, and the divine protector of mankind. The two kings were responsible for overseeing matters of religious, judicial, and military nature. They were deemed the highest priests of the state of Sparta and maintained close contact with the Delphian sanctuary, a separate entity which had always had a hand in Spartan political issues. In 450 B.C., the ruling of the kings were limited to heiresses, adoptions and public roads, described by the famous rhetorician Isocrates (not to be confused with Socrates) as "subject to an oligarchy at home, to a kingship on campaign" (Niebuhr Tod, *The Encyclopædia Britannica*[5]).

A group of individuals known as the ephors (also known as gerousia or "council of elders") took on the state's civil and criminal law cases. The gerousia was the Spartan council of elders consisting of men over the age of sixty and was initiated by the Spartan lawmaker Lycurgus in his Great Rhetra ("Great Proclamation") during the seventh century B.C. This council of elders consisted of twenty-eight men over the age of sixty. Once a man was elected as a member of the ephors, he would remain in the position for life and often he would reside in the home or royalty serving the two kings. The ephor would discuss what modern-day Americans would refer to as "hot button issues" in politics and they would propose alternative solutions to the damos, the masses of Spartan citizens, who would vote for the solution of their choice.

To clarify the term "damos," it is necessary to understand that not all inhabitants of Sparta were classified as citizens. In order to be accepted as a citizen, one must have to pass a Spartan education process known as "agoge" (meaning leading, guidance, and training). All male Spartan men were required to undergo this process with the exception of the first son born to either of the royal families. The agoge process

---

[5] Niebuhr Tod, Marcus. "Sparta," *The Encyclopædia Britannica: A Dictionary of Arts, Sciences, Literature and General Information*, Encyclopædia Britannica, Inc., London 1911, 11:611

involved stealth training, earning the loyalty of the Spartans, combat training, hunting, dancing, singing, and communication. Usually the only inhabitants of Sparta who were qualified to take on the agoge process were direct descendants of the original inhabitants of the society. Non-citizens of Sparta included the perioikoi, who roamed the city freely, and the state-owned slaves known as the helots. Inhabitants of Sparta who were not direct descendants of the original Spartans were not eligible for agoge and Spartans who could not afford the fees associated with the agoge would be in jeopardy of losing their citizenship.

Birth and Death

Because Sparta was a predominantly military state, the Spartan men were often busy training for combat or away in battle and, therefore, they had to enlist a class of slaves called Helots to perform any necessary manual labor within the society. The moment a newborn Spartan was brought into the world, it would almost immediately be trained in physical fitness techniques, especially if the child was a boy.

Not long after birth, a mother would traditionally place her newborn in a tub of wine to analyze its strength. If the child survived the wine bath, it would be brought to the Gerousia by child's father. This council of elders would decide whether the child should continue to be parented. As it noteworthy regarding these birthing rituals, the Spartans were likely one of the first groups of people to have an early method of eugenics. If the council of elders decided that the child was too small or possessed a deformity, it is believed that the child would be tossed into an abyss on Mount Taygetos, known to the Spartans as the Apothetae (a Greek word meaning "Deposits"). While the Spartans are considered to stand out in this respect by some historians, evidence has been acquired supporting that other societies in ancient Greece also practiced discarding children who did not meet the approval of adults. Furthermore, the primitive practice of eugenics in Sparta remains controversial since, to date, only adult bodily remains have been discovered.

Unlike in modern-day western society, a marked headstone on a grave plot was not granted to everyone in Sparta. A marked headstone was earned by soldiers who died in combat during a time of triumph and women who died in service of a sacred institution or during childbirth.

Women and Marriage

As previously stated, Spartan women were unique to ancient Greece in that they were known for being fairly open-minded and were allowed more privileges and power in their society. Women were able to own and manage buildings and were typically free from the burden of domestic duties such as cooking, cleaning, and constructing clothing as these were jobs filled by the Helots. Although the women were not permitted to serve in the military, they did receive an education similar to that of their male counterparts which included studying reading, writing, music, and dancing. However, in order to court men, women often participated in athletic competitions such as javelin-throwing (a javelin is a spear-like shaft that is usually made of wood) or wrestling in addition to singing and dancing contests.

Marriage and procreation were an important part of Spartan life because the council placed pressure on couples to produce male children who could join the ranks of the Spartan military on the battlefield. The Spartans firmly understood the concept of strength in numbers and relied on male children to replace warriors who died in combat. The wedding and marriage customs of the Spartans may seem peculiar to us now, but they were a society with strict traditions and a heavy focus on family. While many ancient cultures would marry girls between the ages of twelve and thirteen years of age, Sparta had a law against young women marrying prior to their early twenties. The rationality behind such a law was to ensure that Spartan women birthed healthy children and to prevent women from experiencing the deathly complications often associated with child rearing before their bodies had been fully developed.

In order to prepare for her wedding day, a Spartan woman would have her head shaved to the scalp by a bridesmaid and would maintain short hair during the extent of her marriage. It is believed by some that the shaving of the woman's head symbolizes her passage into a new stage of life and that the woman was dressed in men's clothing because men, spending most of their lives among other men in the military, were somewhat oblivious to typical expectations regarding a woman's appearance. In addition, the bridesmaid dressed the bride in a cloak and sandals meant for a man and laid her across a mattress in the dark for the groom. The groom, who was to remain sober in order to avoid impotence, would dine with the wedding guests and then slip away to meet his bride and consummate their marriage.

Unlike traditional monogamous couples in the modern western world, married Spartans would live in separate homes since men under the age of thirty were expected to continue inhabiting the military barracks. The only way for men to spend time with their wives during their term of service would be to sneak out of the barracks and return before being caught.

Women's Roles in Spartan Society

Contrary to many ancient cultures around the world, Spartan women possessed great status, power, and were respected citizens of the Sparta society. Beginning from the time that a Spartan woman was born she would hold many of the same rights and privileges as her male counterparts. Young Spartan girls were allowed to exercise, compete in athletic competitions just like young Spartan boys; they were not confined to a future of domestic life as one might expect. The women of Sparta were also highly intelligent in literature and mathematics, which was a rare quality for furthermore, due to the fact that the women of Sparta were restricted from marriage or bearing children before reaching adulthood and that they were well fed and engaged in regular exercise, their bodies maintained in healthier shape and, thus, their life expectancy was longer than that of other Greek women, the average age of death being approximately thirty-five years old.

Although Athenian women wore heavy clothing that hid their bodies from the public eye and were often remained inside their homes, Spartan women draped themselves in dresses with a long slit, which permitted them to move about the city with greater ease either on foot or by chariot.

In addition to their social and intellectual freedoms, the Spartan women exercised economic power since they managed their own properties as well as those of their husbands within the city. Evidence suggests that in the Classical Sparta period, while the male population was falling due to combat-related deaths, women had full ownership of at least thirty-five percent of all property in the city of Sparta, including land. Adding to the Spartan women's socioeconomic power, laws were in place that gave them the same rights as men to divorce.

Despite the Spartans' traditional values of marriage and family, according to visitors of the city, they were also known to engage in "wife sharing," a sort of early form of artificial insemination. With a focus on passing along the genes of the most physically fit Spartans, many older men who struggled with impotency would enlist the assistance of younger more physically fit men to procreate with their wives. Men who had failed to marry or procreate could ask for the permission to impregnate the wife of another man if she had a reputation as a promising child bearer in order to carry on his legacy as a warrior. Because of these procreation practices, Spartan women have often been considered to be polygamous (Greek word meaning "married to multiple spouses"). Due to the Spartans' continuous involvement in battle through their years as a society, this practice was encouraged in order for women to produce many strong children to repopulate Sparta after frequent declines combat-related deaths.

Chapter 2:
Becoming a Spartan Warrior

Spartan Combat Training and Tradition

Many ancient Greek societies such as Athens were heavily focused on visual and performing arts, intellect, and philosophy; however, Sparta was a Mecca for warriors training to shed blood, sweat, and tears in battle. While Spartan women maintained more freedom, the only future for a Spartan man was to live and die with his spear in one hand and his sword in the other.

Once a Spartan by was proven to be physically fit, he faced a future filled with much struggling but if he remained focused on his destiny as a solder, the means would have an honorable end. Spartan boys would spend the first few years of their lives with their parents or their mother and a helot housekeeper but were primed to ponder the military training ahead of them. They would begin their training at the early age of seven years old, when they left home and started the process of Agoge, which was a process that would reiterate the values of Spartan culture. The boys would live under one roof communally where they were divided into groups. While in these training quarters, Spartan boys lived under rigorous conditions, being forced to participate in constant physical competitions involving brutality and violence, offered minimal food portions and were expected to learn a number of combat survival skills including strategies for stealing provisions. The education and training of the boys would be structured with different levels of difficulty based on age, with the first phase of training ranging from six and seven year-olds to seventeen year-olds, then eighteen to twenty year-olds, and after the age of twenty the training would continue until the now men reached the age of twenty-nine or thirty when they were allowed more freedom and rights as citizens.

Teenage boys who showed the most promise on the battlefield and displayed quality leadership skills were chosen to take part in the Crypteia, which was a sort of private police force that maintained a primary goal of antagonizing the general population of helots and killing those who would not follow orders. By the age of twenty years old, Spartan men were deemed full-fledged warriors and would stay on active duty until they reached the age of sixty years old.

In the first phase of their education and training, the Spartan boys would move into their new homes in the military-style barracks with a simplistic look, where they would reside with other boys in their age group. During the second phase, the Spartan boys would become reserve members of the armed forces of the state of Sparta. Although they were not yet classified among the adult male warriors, they would still be enlisted to assist the men on the battlefield in times of dire need. If the boys were not requested to join the troops of soldiers in battle during this phase, they also had the chance to be assigned to a guard as part of the Spartan secret police force. In the third phase of this intense process, when the boys reached the age of twenty years old, the Spartan boys would be accepted into one of many public messes called "syssitia," a type of dining club, through an act of voting, the already existing members of these public messes holding complete power over who is to enter their group. The boys were allowed up to ten years to collaborate with the public messes and earn their acceptance to ensure that they would be voted into the group of their choice.

These public messes each consisted of approximately fifteen members, and each Spartan male citizen was required to join one of them. It was within these public messes that the young Spartan men learned to live as brothers and rely on one another for help when needed. The Spartans were not eligible to become elected members of office until the age of thirty years old. Furthermore, only native Spartans were eligible to become citizens and participate in the training required by law to become warriors of the state of Sparta, and only native Spartans were permitted to join and financially contribute to any of the public messes. Once selected to become a member of an officer's mess, the Spartan man will spend most of the remainder of his life there only to leave from time to time after marriage to fulfill his requirements of a conjugal life.

Sparta is believed to be the first society to ever popularize athletic training in the nude, as the Spartans were confident that the love of an older noble for a teenage boy was necessary to his transformation into a free citizen. The agoge, the education part of a Spartan boy's upbringing, made this aristocratic lover responsible for the boy's training, although this assumption regarding Spartan culture remains in question.

The Spartans' continuous military drills and punishment of the unruly prepared young boys to become skilled at fighting style unique to ancient Greek culture called phalanx formation, a type of combat involving military forces using armor, shields, and long spears. In this phalanx style of combat, the military troop worked as one solid unit, remaining close together and displaying well-coordinated maneuvers in unison. With the exception of the leading general, all soldiers on the battlefield were believed to be equal, lacking specific ranks. Once on the battlefield, an armed solder, which was referred to as a "hoplite," adorned a massive bronze helmet over his head, breastplate armor and ankle guards in addition to a red cloak, and he carried a large round shield constructed from bronze and wood on his arm and he maintained a tight grip on a long wooden spear in his other hand.

Spartan men were pressured to marry at the age of twenty years old but were not permitted to live under the same roof as their wives until they were relieved of their active duty in the armed forces at the age of thirty years old. Despite no longer being an active member of duty at the age of thirty years old, Spartan men still remained as members of the reserve until the age of sixty years old.

While Spartan women were not allowed to participate in military training, they did play a minor role in the cultural rites of passage for men becoming full-time soldiers of the state of Sparta. Thucydides claimed that before a Spartan man left for war, his wife or another significant woman in his life would present him with his shield known as a hoplon and recite the words "With this or upon this," which meant that only a true Spartan would possess the power to return to Sparta either alive with triumphant with their shield still intact on their arm ("with this") or dead ("up this") (Plutarch, *Moralia*[6]). Of course, this traditional phrase was mostly meant to act as political propaganda during war times seeing as the Spartans typically buried their deceased on or near the battle grounds; the remains of fallen soldiers were not carried back to their homes in Sparta. According to Spartan tradition, it was considered less honorable for a Spartan soldier to lose his hoplon than his helmet, breastplate armor, or ankle guards because the hoplon was designed to not only protect him in battle but to also protect the soldier to his left. Therefore, the

---

[6] Plutarch, Frank Cole Babbit, ed., *Moralia Vol. III*, Loeb Classical Library, Cambridge: Harvard University Press, 2004

hoplon was meant to be symbolic of a Spartan soldier's subservience to his fellow brothers in his military unit, his role in the success of his troop, and his dedication to his armed comrades who were often of blood relation.

According to the Greek philosopher Aristotle, the Spartan military ethics were short-sighted and ineffectual. He stated, "It is the standards of civilized men not of beasts that must be kept in mind, for it is good men not beasts who are capable of real courage. Those like the Spartans who concentrate on the one and ignore the other in their education turn men into machines and in devoting themselves to one single aspect of the city's life, end up making them inferior even in that" (Forrest, A History of Sparta[7]). Aristotle may have had a valid point, but it is important to bear in mind that he was also known to be a tough critic of Spartan culture and political policies. In addition, there is evidence in existence from the archaic period that suggests that the Spartans were not as narrowly educated as Aristotle assumed, as they also received a thorough education in logic and philosophy.

Spartan Military Tactical Techniques

Similar to other armed forces in ancient Greek city-states, the Spartan armed forces were an infantry-focused organization that battled using the popular phalanx formation. The earliest known display of the phalanx formation of fighting occurred in a Sumerian stone from the 25th century B.C. Although historians are in disagreement regarding the precise relationship between the phalanx formation and the overall

---

[7] Forrest, W.G. A History of Sparta, 950-192 B.C., New York: W. W. Norton & Co. 1968

Greek formation as well as other predecessors of the hoplites, the principles and basic features of the shield wall and spear hedge appear to be universal among all armies incorporating this method of battle. Most historians tend to date the use of the hoplite phalanx formation back to 8th century B.C. ancient Greece in the city-state of Sparta. However, there has been some speculation that the phalanx military tactics could have gone further back to the 7th century B.C. after the introduction of the hoplon in Argos. Another theory regarding the phalanx formation in ancient Greece refers to the possibility that some of the basic techniques used in phalanx formation were apparent in the early years of the Spartans but were still in development due to the still progressing technology.

The hoplite phalanx formation used by Spartans in the Archaic and Classical Sparta time periods (ca. 750-350 B.C.) was a method in which the hoplites would stand in a line in close proximity of one another, their shields interlocking and the first few rows of warriors would launch their spears over the first row of shields. In practicing this strategy, the hoplites would create a wall with their shields to protect them from their enemies with their spears aimed toward their enemies, making it easier for them to avoid being attacked from the front. It also permitted many soldiers to engage in combat simultaneously, side by side.

Most phalanx formation battles occurred on flat solid ground where it was more convenient to remain in a perfect line with fellow soldiers and advance on the battlefield. Land that consisted of hills or rough terrain would make it difficult for the phalanx to maintain in a straight line. Because so many Greek city-states included this method of combat in their war time tactics, they ensured that all battles were initiated on flatlands allowing for a fair fight to the death or—more often than not—a fair fight until one side decided to retreat.

25

The phalanx formation typically moved forward across the battlefield at a walking pace or a march, although it is likely that they increased their speed in the final few yards of the battle ground to gain momentum against their enemy upon first contact all the while trying not to lose its straight line shape and be rendered ineffective. The Greek historian Herodotus reported that "They [the Spartans] were the first Greeks [at the Battle of Marathon, that] we know of to charge their enemy at a run" (Herodotus, *The History*[8]). Many historians have theorized that the Spartans used this running technique in order to keep their losses from Persian archery to a minimum. With this tactic, both opposing sides would collide into each other which would likely kill a large portion of the front rank of warriors due to the bone crushing caused by the collision. Therefore, the front rank of soldiers tended to have the most vigorous role on the battlefield while the ranks in the back would continue to hold their shields at their chests, pressing them up against the ranks in front for support and protection. When in combat, the entire phalanx formation would move forward in this manner with shields pressed against the row in front of them in an effort to disrupt the perfect formation of the enemy, thus, when contact was made between enemies, it essentially initiated a pushing match.

Pushing

The "physical pushing match" theory is the most widely accredited theory regarding Spartan military combat

---

[8] Herodotus. *The History*, trans. David Grene, Chicago: University of Chicago Press, 1987, 454

techniques (Hanson, *The Western Way of War*[9]). American military historian Victor Davis Hanson has pointed out that it is not easy to account for a solid phalanx formation unless they were used to coordinate the physical act of pushing as explained in the theory seeing as the first couple ranks toward the front would not be able to participate in spear throwing.

Shields

It was customary for each individual Spartan hoplite to bear his shield on his left arm so that he would not only protect himself in battle but he could also protect the soldier to the left of him. Unfortunately, this meant that the soldiers standing to the extreme right were far less protected compared to the rest of the troops and the enemy would often use this weakness to their advantage by attempting to outnumber the right side of the ranks. However, likely to the opposing phalanx's surprise, some groups in ancient Greece such as the Spartans most experienced soldiers were often placed at the far right side of the ranks in the formation to avoid compromise of the phalanx. The downside of this strategy, however, is that now the left side of each rank, which was usually made up of soldiers from allied troops, would now be in a vulnerable situation, thus, it was probably rare that this technique often proved to be successful.

Each row of the phalanx included a leader as well as a rear officer called the ouragos (Greek word meaning "tall leader") who maintained order in the back of the phalanx. The phalanx

---

[9] Hanson, Victor Davis. *The Western Way of War: Infantry Battle in Classical Greece*, Berkeley, Los Angeles, and London, University of California Press 1989

formation is a prime early example of a military technique in which conformity is heavily encouraged for the greater good of the ranks as a whole. Because of the way in which the phalanx formation was designed, the hoplites were forced to trust in their neighboring soldiers for protection and they had to be willing to protect the their neighbors in return, causing the technique to fall in line with the timeless military motto that a troop is only as strong as its weakest link. Therefore, the hoplites' potential for victory in times of war depended on their ability to remain obedient in phalanx formation as well as their physical strength and sense of strong will. The Spartans were also wise in that they typically grouped family and friends close together within the same ranks because they knew that their soldiers would likely make a bigger effort to protect their loved ones than complete strangers and that soldiers who attempted to run and hide would be more likely to be shamed by their peers. More often than not, one side or the other would eventually forfeit and flee the battlefield, allowing their opponent an automatic victory. Ancient Greeks often referred to the word dynamis, which meant the "will to fight," to express the motivation and drive of their warriors.

The Spartan poet Tyrtaeus once wrote, "Now of those, who dare, abiding one beside the other, to advance to the close fray, and the foremost champions, fewer die, and they save the people in the rear; but in men that fear, all excellence is lost. No one could ever in words go through those several ills, which befall a man, if he has been actuated by cowardice. For 'tis grievous to wound in the rear the back of a flying man in a hostile war" (Tyrtæus, *The Idylls*[10]).

---

[10] Tyrtæus, Theocritus, Bion, Moschus. *The Idylls of Theocritus, Bion and Moschus, and the War Songs of Tyrtæus*

Hoplite Armament

Each hoplite in the Spartan armed forces was responsible for equipping themselves with their own weapons. The most common weapon used by a hoplite was a spear called a "dory" which was about 7.9 feet in length. It was held in one hand while the other hand carried the hoplite's shield, which was called "Aspis." The head of the spear was typically curved and in the shape of a leaf and the end of the spear contained a spike called a sauroter (meaning "lizard killer") which was used to plant the spear into the ground. In addition, it was used as a secondary weapon in case the main shaft of the spear broke in half or to kill soldiers from the opposing side lying on the ground as their phalanx formation marched forward.

Through the various periods of Spartan history, the armor worn by the hoplites went through a number of changes. During the archaic period, for example, hoplites often wore a bronze breastplate, a bronze helmet complete with cheek plates, and greaves (metal shin guards). However, in the classical Sparta period, the breastplate became less typical dress for soldiers and was replaced with a corselet that was believed to be made of layers of linen fabric pieces that had been glued together or possibly of made of leather scraps sometimes completely or partially covered by with metal scales which overlapped each other. As time went on, the greaves also became less common for Spartan soldiers to be seen wearing and were gradually replaced by heavier armor. This evolution of the armor worn by soldiers was a reflection of the changing times and the attempt to find the balance between

---

trans. The Rev. J. Banks, M.A. London: George Bell and Sons, 1878 being able to move across a battlefield with ease and remaining protection from injury or death.

Deployment into the Battlefield

The composition and strength of a phalanx competition varied depending on the city-state; however, the most basic types of phalanx formation were the stichos (Greek word meaning "file," traditionally consisting of 8-16 men) and the enomotia (Greek word meaning "sworn," traditionally consisting of a maximum of 32 men). Both types of phalanx formations were led by dimoerites who was accompanied by a decadarchos and two decasteroe. Between 4 and 32 enomotiae (depending on the time period and the city-state) would form a lochos (or tactical sub unit of the phalanx formation) led by a lochagos who essentially had command of around 100 hoplites and sometimes up to 500 hoplites during the late Hellenistic period. The Spartans specifically held the standard of "mora," which was the highest standard of hoplitic phalanx formation consisting of 500 to 1500 men led by a general called the strategos. As a whole, the armed forces were ruled by a general's council and the commander-in-chief of the hoplites was called either polemarchos or a strategos autocrator.

Hoplite phalanx usually deployed for combat in groups of 8 or more soldiers deep with the exception of more extreme battle situations such as the Battle of Leuctra which you will read about more in-depth in a later chapter. The depth of the hoplite phalanx formation depended on the need of the armed forces at a given time of war and the plans laid out by the hoplite general.

Stages of Spartan Combat

The following are the five stages of hoplite combat defined:

- *Ephodos*: During this stage, the hoplites cease their singing of their paeanes (Greek word translated as "battle hymns) and advance toward the enemy, gradually increasing their speed and momentum. In the time before impact is made, the soldiers would let out war cries.

- *Krousis*: The opposing phalanx formation make physical contact nearly simultaneously along the front lines of the battlefield. The promachoe (what the Greeks called the front-liners) were expected to not only be physically fit but psychologically fit as well to avoid the potential for second-guessing or wavering decisions in combat. Often times, the men placed in the front row were experienced veterans.

- *Doratismos*: This stage of combat was defined by repeatedly rapid spear thrusting in order to create chaos in the phalanx formation of the enemy. The advantage of using longer spears was that they could successfully separate the opposing formation's hoplites to keep them from assisting the soldiers next to them. This prodding of the opposing formation also worked to leave individual opponents vulnerable to being easily speared. However, it was important that the soldiers did not use their spears to prod too forcefully so that they would not get their spears stuck in shields.

- *Othismus*: Literally meaning "pushing," this stage begins after most soldiers had broken their spears and would begin to shove their enemies with what was left

31

of their spears. This was typically the longest phase of combat.

- *Pararrhexis*: The Greek word meaning "breaching" the enemy, this stage of the basic combat procedure signifies the shattering of the opposing hoplite phalanx formation and the end of the battle. At this time, the cavalry would scatter across the battlefield to pick up the bodies of the fallen soldiers.

Chapter 3:
Battle of Thermopylae

The Battle of Thermopylae was fought by the league of Greek city-states, which was led by King Leonidas of the city-state of Sparta, and the Persian Empire of Xerxes I, lasting a total of three days as part of the second invasion of Greece by Persia. At the same time, the battle at Artemisium was taking place at sea in 480 B.C. The invasion of Greece was a late response by the Persians to the initial failure of their first invasion, which was ended by victorious Athenians during the Battle of Marathon in 490 B.C. Xerxes I prepared for the Battle of Thermopylae by assembling massive naval and army troops as he made plans to conquer Greece.

The Greeks gathered together an armed force of 7,000 warriors who marched north to block the Persians from entering their territory during the summer of 480 B.C. However, it is believed by historians that the Persians greatly outnumbered the Greeks with naval and army troops consisting of approximately 100,000 to 150,000 men strong who appeared at the Greek pass in either August or September of that year. Although the Greeks were outnumbered by the Persians, they were able to keep the Persians at bay for about seven days including the three days of battle before the rear guard of the Greek armed forces was murdered in one of the most well-known last stands in the history of the world. During the first two days of the Battle of Thermopylae, the small group of Greek soldiers were led by King Leonidas to block off the only path available to the Persians to begin an invasion. On the third day, however, a Greek local named Ephialtes was disloyal to the Greeks as he revealed to the Persians that there was a small trail that led behind the Greek border. Aware that his armed forces were being outnumbered sent away many Greek soldiers and stayed to keep watch on their retreat with 300 of the finest Spartans, 700 Thespians, 400 Thebans, and quite possibly a few hundred other Greeks, most of whom died in battle.

Background on the Battle of Thermopylae

Two Greek city-states, Athens and Eretria, had encouraged the failed Ionian Revolt against the Persian Empire ruled by Darius I from 499 to 494 B.C. when the Persian Empire was still developing and vulnerable to revolts against Darius's rulings. As predicted, Darius spent much of his time as king extinguishing the flames of revolt by his subjects. The Ionian Revolt in particular destroyed much of the credibility of his empire and Darius was determined to discipline anyone with any involvement in the revolt, especially the Athenians since he was positive that the Ionians would not get aware with their rebellion without facing the consequences. Ambitious as he was, Darius considered a possible invasion of Greece as an opportunity to stretch his territory further than the borders of the Persian Empire. In order to get the ball rolling on his idea, Darius sent emissaries to all the major Greek city-states in 491 B.C. to request a gift of "earth and water" as a token of their obedience to him. Previously demonstrating the depths of his power just one year prior to this, most Greek city-states voluntarily yielded to this agreement. But the ambassadors in Athens were reluctant to follow suit and were put on trial only to be executed by being thrown into a large pit. The Spartans also refused to go along with Darius and his emissaries and, thus, they were pushed down a well. This signified war between Sparta and the Persian Empire.

In response to the Athenians and the Spartans lack of cooperation, Darius enlisted a task force led by his nephew Artephernes and admiral Datis in 490 B.C., which was instructed to attack Naxos. The task force later moved on to destroy Eretria before returning to Athens at the bay of Marathon and was surprised by the Athenian armed forces. The Athenians saw a great victory at the Battle of Marathon which led the Persian armed forces to run away to Asia.

Learning from his mistakes in the previous invasion attempt, Darius constructs new bigger armed forces troop in order to completely dominate ancient Greece. Unfortunately for Darius, in 486 B.C., his Egyptian subjects began to rebel against him, which delayed his invasion of Greece. Darius soon died while preparing to march into Egypt for a confrontation and the kingship over Persia was passed down to Xerxes I. Continuing the work that Darius started, Xerxes stomped out the revolt in Egypt and proceeded to prepare for an invasion of ancient Greece. Due to the fact that this invasion was meant to be a full-scale one, it was necessary to set long-term goals and plan ahead, store provisions, and enlist as many soldiers as possible to join in this battle. In order to safeguard his territory, Xerxes made the decision to create a bridge over Hellespont, a waterway northwest of Turkey, and that a large hole should be dug along Mount Athos in order for his armed forces to have a way to cross over Europe. Both rather ambitious projects were completed by early 480 B.C. and the armed forces of the Persian Empire began to march toward Europe.

What Darius and the Persians did not know, however, was that the Athenians had also been taking measures to prepare for an invasion of their country since the middle of 480 B.C. and by 482 B.C., the Athenians were working toward building three triremes, or large battleships, necessary for fighting off the

Persians. Unfortunately for the Athenians, they did not have enough men to divide into battles over both land and sea, and this is why the Athenians needed to seek the assistance of other city-states in ancient Greece. While Athenians reached out to their neighboring city-states, the emissaries of the Persian Empire were making their rounds across Greece with the deliberate exclusion of Athens and Sparta. As a result of the Athenians' and Spartans' refusal to support Darius and the Persian Empire, other Greek city-states began to follow suit. A congress of the Greek city-states held a meeting at Corinth toward the end of autumn in 481 B.C. and an alliance between Greek city-states was established. This alliance possessed the power to send envoys to request assistance and to enlist troops from neighboring states to consult with them and stand along the defense lines of battle. Considering how fragmented ancient Greece was at this time, it was a monumental movement for Greek city-states to offer each other support considering the fact that many were still somewhat at war with one another.

This Greek congress met once again during the spring of 480 B.C. and a Thessalian delegate offered the suggestion that the Greeks could gather in Vale of Tempe, a gorge along the borders of Thessaly, giving them the advantage to block Xerxes and his men from invading Greece. An armed force of approximately 10,000 hoplites was deployed to the Vale of Tempe, where they were certain that the Persian Empire's armed forces would be required to pass. Alexander I of Macedon was concerned that the blockage of the vale was not a full-proof plan and that the Persians would find a way to bypass it through Sarantoporo Pass, so the Greek armed forces retreated from this plan. It was not much later that the news spread across the Greek city-states that Xerxes and his army of men had passed through the Hellespont.

In an effort to reevaluate the situation at hand, Themistocles came up with a new strategy for the Greeks to come out victorious. The trail to the southern region of Greece (Boeotia, Attica, and the Peloponnese) would force the Persian army of Xerxes to pass through the very narrow path of Thermopylae. This region could easily be blocked off by the Greek hoplites no matter if they were outnumbered by the Persians. In addition, in order to keep the Persian army from bypassing Thermopylae by crossing the sea, the Athenian navy along with its allies could close off the straits of Artemisium. After much discussion of this plan, it received the seal of approval from the Greek congress and the Greek city-states began working toward executing the plan. However, the cities located within the Peloponnese such as Sparta concentrated on a plan B in order to protect the Isthmus of Corinth in case the battle against the Persians escalated. Meanwhile, the women and children of Athens had been evacuated out of the city-state for safety and sought refuge in the Peloponnese city of Troezen.

Prelude to the Battle of Thermopylae

As the Persian armed forces made their way through ancient Greece, they seemed to be making slow progress as they entered Thrace and Macedon. Unlike the progress made by the Persians, news of their invasion approach traveled fast through the Greek city-states which were due in large part to a Greek spy. During this time, the Spartans armed forces as well as their military leaders were celebrating the festival of Carneia, a celebration which focused on Apollo, and Spartan law stated that there should not be any military activity permitted at the time of such a festival. Thus, the Spartans showed up late to the battlefield during the Battle of Marathon. At this time, the Olympic Games were also taking place, and because of this, it would have been doubly blasphemous for the Spartans to leave for battle during such an occasion. Finally, the ephors that assisted the two kings in leading the Spartans confirmed that the situation at Marathon was too severe and that the Spartan armed forces should deploy at once to assist in blocking the pass under the rule of King Leonidas I. King Leonidas was accompanied by 300 men who served as royal bodyguards and were called the Hippeis. The objective of this mission to Marathon was to gather as many Greek warriors as possible until the arrival of the main Spartan armed forces.

The ancient Greek historian Herodotus reported that the Spartans sought answers from the Oracle of Delphi earlier that year, according to Thermopylae legend:

"O ye men who dwell in the streets of broad Lacedaemon!

Honor the festival of the Carneia!! Otherwise,

Either your glorious town shall be sacked by the children of Perseus,

Or, in exchange, must all through the whole Laconian country

Mourn for the loss of a king, descendant of great Heracles" (Herodotus, *The History*[11]).

According to Herodotus, as the prophecy of the Oracle of Delphi predicted, Leonidas was convinced that he was going to die in battle because he believed that his forces were not capable of a victory, thus, he intentionally enlisted Spartans

---

[11] Herodotus. *The History* trans. George Rawlinson, New York: D. Appleman and Company, 1885, 4:7

with living sons so that their legacies would live on should they die on the battlefield with him. The Spartan armed forces were deployed to Thermopylae from various city-states and consisted of more than 7,000 men by the time that they arrived at their destination. Leonidas elected to set up camp at the "middle gate," which was the narrowest region of Thermopylae and was near a defensive wall that was constructed long ago by the Phocians. Soon after settling at Thermopylae, Leonidas received news from the neighboring city of Trachis that there was a mountain pass that the Persians could use to bypass Thermopylae. In order to resolve the hole in the Greeks' initial plan, Leonidas enlisted 1,000 Phoncians to stand guard atop the mountain to block the Persians from entering.

As the middle of August approached, the Persian army was finally spotted across Malian Gulf on their way toward Thermopylae. With the approach of the Persian armed forces at Thermopylae, the Greeks began their battle cries. A few Peloponnesians, concerned about the potential for victory, proposed a withdrawal from the battlefield to the Isthmus of Corinth, which would block the entry way to Peloponnesus. The neighboring Phocians and Locrians, on the other hand, were determined to defend Thermopylae to the death and request for more assistance. Leonidas kept the peace among the Greek hoplites by standing by them to defend Thermopylae.

The conflict at Thermopylae escalating, Xerxes decided to send an emissary to communicate with Leonidas in the hopes of a compromise. Xerxes offered the Greeks a return to freedom and would deem them the "Friends of the Persian People" in addition to being relocated to better quality land than that which they already owned. However, these offers were denied by Leonidas when he was handed a written negotiation from

Xerxes himself which requested that the Greeks forfeit their weapons. Leonidas responded with what has become a famous wise-crack in the history of the world:

Come and take them" (Plutarch, *Moralia*[12]). As the Persian emissary returned to the Persian Empire empty-handed, the progression toward battle was undeniable. Hesitant to take drastic measures, Xerxes waited four days to see if the Greeks would retreat before concluding that a war would begin.

Battle of Thermopylae

Day One

Following the fifth day of the Persians' arrival at Thermopylae in addition to the first official day of battle, Xerxes finally resorted to an attack on the Greeks. First, he demanded that the Persians' five thousand archers launched their arrows but they were unsuccessful when launched from around 100 yards away from their opponents as the arrows seemed to be no match for the Greek hoplites' bronze shields and plate armor. When the attempts with the arrows failed, Xerxes ordered ten thousand Medes and Cissian soldiers to take Greek soldiers as prisoners of war and bring them to him. Next, the Persian armed forces initiated an assault on the Greeks from the front of the line, 10,000 men at a time. The Greeks chose to fight their battles next to the Phocian wall which allowed them to use the services of fewer soldiers than they would have in any other battle. The Greek historian Diodorus reported that "the

---

[12] Plutarch, "Apophthegmata Laconica" *Moralia* trans. Frank Cole Babbit, ed. *Moralia* Vol. III Loeb Classical Library, Cambridge: Harvard University Press, 2004

men stood shoulder to shoulder" and the Greeks were "superior in valor and in the great size of their shields," referring to the phalanx formation strategy popular among ancient Greek military forces (Diodorus, *Diodorus of Sicily*[13]). It was true, in fact, that the Persians possessed weaker shields and smaller spears and swords, which required them to assault the Greeks at a dangerously close range. According to Herodotus, the soldiers from each Greek city-state were kept together as a unit and each unit would take turns entering the battle grounds to participate in combat in order to avoid fatigue of any single unit, which gives an idea of the abundance of the Greek armed forces. Each Greek city-state represented demonstrated somewhat unique battle tactics to their training with the Spartans practicing their classic forging a retreat before performing an about face and annihilating their enemy.

Day Two

On the next day of the Battle of Thermopylae, Xerxes sent in another troop of soldiers to attack the Greeks at the pass, assuming that their enemy was too wounded to continue fighting back. However, as history often tends to repeat itself, the Persian armed forces once again were unsuccessful in their attempted assaults on the Greeks. Frustrated by the failed attempts, Xerxes retreated to his tent on the side lines of the battlefield.

---

[13] Diodorus Siculus. *Diodorus of Sicily in Twelve Volumes* trans. C. H. Oldfather Vol 4-8 Cambridge, Mass.: Harvard University Press; London: William Heinemann, Ltd. 1989

Later on in the same day, Xerxes was contemplating alternative tactics in his tent when he received a piece of good fortune, a Trachinian named Ephialtes told him of a mountain pass which would allow him to bypass Thermopylae to get to the Greeks. In fact, Ephialtes offered to give Xerxes as well as the Persian army a guided tour of the mountain pass with the hope that he would receive a reward of some kind in return. Since Ephialtes was willing to help the Persian enemy, he went down in history as the ultimate traitor to the Greeks and his name evolved to be synonymous with the Greek word for "nightmare." Herodotus had reported that Xerxes sent Hydarnes, his military commander of the Immortals, to have the Greeks surrounded via the mountain pass without telling Hydarnes who the men were that he wanted surrounded. Hydarnes enlisted 20,000 men to take on this mission.

Day Three

By dawn on the third and final day of the Battle of Thermopylae, the Phocians who were standing guard at the mountain pass took notice of the Persian soldiers arriving by the rustling of leaves. At first, the Persians feared that the Phocians standing guard might be Spartans but Ephialtes assured them that the Phocians were not Spartans. The Phocians ran to a nearby hill to prepare their plan of a counterattack against the Persians. Not wasting any time, the Persians immediately began shooting dozens of arrows in the direction of the Phocians before finally bypassing them to attack the main Greek military force.

Upon receiving the news that the Phocians had not held up the fort at the mountain pass, Leonidas requested a council of war at sunrise. Although some Greek soldiers begged for a withdrawal from the battle, Leonidas insisted on remaining at the pass alongside the Spartans. Many Greek city-states chose to retreat from the battle individually against the orders of Leonidas or were requested to leave the battlefield by Leonidas himself. Despite the vast number of soldiers deciding to flee the battlefield, 700 Thespians who were led by their general Demophilus were determined to continue fighting. In addition, 400 Thebans also chose to stay in battle as well as the Spartans and possibly some Helots.

Although it is often claimed by historians that the Spartans did not retreat from the battlefield due to the laws of Sparta, it is possible that the Spartans earned the reputation of never retreating because of their failure to retreat while at Thermopylae. Furthermore, it is also likely that Leonidas was determined to take his own life for the sake of Sparta as a self-fulfilling prophecy after hearing the words of the Oracle of Delphi.

At sunrise, Xerxes permitted the Immortals enough time to make their way up the mountain pass before advancing toward the Greeks himself. Ten thousand members of the Persian armed forces, which consisted of light infantry as well as cavalry, charged at the front ranks of the Greek phalanx formation. Unlike the last couple days, all of the Greeks now fled from the wall to charge the Persians in an effort to annihilate as many members of the Persian armed forces as possible. When all spears were shattered and broken, the Greek warriors would switch to short swords to kill their enemy. Shot by Persian archers, Leonidas died in combat as predicted in the oracle and both the Persians and the Greeks fought over the king's body lying on the battle ground until the Greeks finally carried him away. Once the Immortals approached, the Greeks retreated behind the Phocian-built wall. As he tore apart a portion of the wall, Xerxes demanded that the hill upon which the wall stood be surrounded by his troops. The pass at Thermopylae now wide open for Persian access, the Persian army was down by approximately 20,000 men.

Aftermath of the Battle of Thermopylae

When Xerxes received word that the Persians discovered the body of Leonidas on the battle ground, he—in a tyrannical state—demanded that the head be removed and the body crucified. This sort of treatment of a corpse was supposedly unlike the Persians, according to Herodotus, as they typically treated fallen warriors with honor and respect. However, Xerxes had a reputation for his uncontrollable rage and, according to legend, it is believed that he ordered Hellespont (yes, a body of water) to be whipped because it would not cooperate with him. After the invasion of Greece had ceased, a stone lion monument was put into place in memory of King Leonidas. The remains of Leonidas, however, were not returned to Sparta and given a proper burial until forty years after the Battle of Thermopylae ended.

It is believed by some that the Battle of Thermopylae was a devastating victory for the Persian Empire since their army appeared to be just as wounded as that of the Greeks. But accounts by Herodotus suggest that this was not the case since the theory ignores the obvious fact that the Persians took over most of Greece and that the Persians continued fighting against the Greeks a year after the battle. One of the most famous moments that took place during the Battle of Thermopylae was that the rear guard stood his ground on the battlefield despite his definite destiny to die in combat.

Chapter 4:
Battle of Plataea

The Battle of Plataea was the last battle fought on land during the second invasion of ancient Greece by Persians. This battle took place during 479 B.C. near the city of Plataea in Boeotia and the conflict lied between the Greek city-states such as Sparta, Athens, Corinth, and Megara and the Persian Empire which was still being led by Xerxes I. During the Battle of Thermopylae just one year prior, the Persian armed forces, led by the then Persian king, had acquired great victories in addition to conquering Thessaly, Boeotia, Euboea, and Attica. However, in the Battle of Salamis which directly followed, the Greek navy alliance came out victorious which protected Peloponnesus from being conquered by the Persians. After this victory by the Greeks, Xerxes retreated along with many of his army soldiers, leaving his general Mardonius behind on the battlefield to finish killing the remainder of the Greek soldiers.

During the summer of 479 B.C., the Greeks mustered a massive army of hoplites and marched out of Peloponnesus. The Persians took refuge in Boeotia and set up a fortified camp site just outside of Plataea. On the other hand, the Greeks avoided being lured into the main cavalry terrain near the Persians' camping grounds, which ended up in a deadlock that went on for eleven days. While plotting a retreat once provision sources were compromised, the Greeks' phalanx formation was disrupted. Assuming the Greeks had already gone into complete retreat, the general Mardonius demanded that the Persian armed forces attack them. Much to the surprise of these Persian troops, the Greeks—mainly the Spartans, Tegeans, and Athenians—stopped and put up a fight, crushing the Persian armed forces and killing Mardonius.

Much of the Persian army soldiers ended up trapped within their camp and annihilated by the Greeks. It was this slaughter as well as that of the Persian naval forces occurring at the same time in the Battle of Mycale which put an end to the invasion of Greece. Following the battles of Plataea and Mycale, the Greek alliance took the offensive stance against the Persians, leading to a new chapter in the Greco-Persian War story. Despite being a resounding victory for the Greeks, the Battle of Plataea seems to carry a different kind of significance compared to the Battle of Marathon in which the Athenians were scored a victory or the Battle of Thermopylae in which the Spartans were sorely defeated.

Prelude to the Battle of Plataea

When the general Mardonius first learned about the Spartan armed forces, he finished destroying Athens by knocking down any building that remained standing. Next, he retreated in the direction of Thebes in hopes of decoying the Greek army into new territory that he believed would be acceptable for the Persian cavalry. Mardonius built an equipped camp settlement on the banks of Asopus River in Boeotia. In response, the Athenians deployed 8,000 men, led by Aristides, as well as 600 Plataean exiles to join forces with the Greek allied army. The army of Athenians and Plataeans marched into Boeotia near Plataea and, under the supervision of commanding General Pausanias, the Greeks lined up opposite the Persians on high ground. Aware that he would be hopeless against the Greeks, Mardonius had to make one of two choices: either disseminate rebellion among the Greek allies or lure them down to the flat land. In addition, Mardonius also acted as an instigator in that he initiated hit-and-run assaults by the Persian cavalry near enemy lines, possibly in attempt to drag the Greeks down to the plain for further attacks. However, the tactic proved unsuccessful when the Persian cavalry commander Masistius was murdered, which became a major deciding factor in the cavalry's plan to retreat.

After the minor victory over the Persians, the Greeks marched onward, staying on higher ground, to a new location better suited for setting up camp as it had a more bountiful water supply. The Spartans and Tegeans stood to the right of the phalanx formation, the Athenians to the left and all other Greek allies on somewhat lower ground in front. To counter the actions of the Greeks, Mardonius led his men to the Asopus and prepared them for battle. Both the Persians and the Greeks, however, refrained from attacking at this time due to bad omens sensed during sacrificial rituals. Both sides remained at their camps for eight days and at this time, the Greeks acquired extra troops. Mardonius was then determined to break the deadlock by ordering his cavalry to initiate an attack on Mount Cithaeron, with the outcome of stolen provisions that were meant to be delivered to the Greeks. With the passing of two more days, the Greeks' provisions continued to be compromised by the Persians. In another menacing attack on the Greeks, the Persians raided the Greeks' supply lines, this time blocking off their water source at Gargaphian Spring. The lack of food and water forced the Greeks to retreat near Plataea where they would have better access to fresh water.

Unfortunately for the Greeks, their retreat did not go according to plan as the allied soldiers in the center of the formation missed their marks and ended up spread out in front of Plataea. The Athenians, Tegeans, and Spartans, who were aligned in the rear of the formation, had not begun their retreat just yet. One division of the Spartan force was, therefore, left behind to protect the back of the formation, retreating further up the hill. Furthermore, the Athenians were ordered by Pausanias to initiate the retreat and meet up with the Spartans. Instead of following instructions, the Athenians at first began to head toward Plataea, further disorganizing the phalanx.

The Battle of Plataea

Once the Persians realized that the Greeks had retreated from their original positions on the hill, Mardonius chose to pursue the Greek armed forces by enlisting an elite Persian infantry, the other Persian troops following behind. By this time, the Spartans and the Tegeans had arrived at the Temple of Demeter. Going against the orders of Pausanias to follow behind the Spartans, the Athenians had been involved with the Theban phalanx formation and, thus, could not assist the Spartans. The Spartans and the Tegeans were the first ranks of the Greek forces to be attacked by the Persian cavalry as the Persian infantry marched forward. After this initial attack, the Persians then laid their shields to rest and began launching arrows toward the Greeks while the cavalry stood back. At this time, the Greek warriors began to duck under the arrows while the Tegeans charged at the Persians' front ranks. Providing one final prayer to the heavens above and a sacrifice near the Temple of Hera, it is believed that the Greeks were finally given good omens and Pausanias ordered the Spartans to continue onward and charge the Persians in line with the Tegeans.

The highest quality Persian infantry was called the sparabara formation; however, it was still no match for the hoplite phalanx formation used by the Greeks. In addition to differing battle tactics, the Persians also used shields made of wicker and short spears compared to the Greeks' bronze shields and longer spears. In an effort to create a fair fight, the Persians attempted to break the Greeks' spears by grabbing them and snapping them in half but the Greeks wisely switched to swords for backup in this situation. Although Mardonius rode in on a white horse across the battlefield with a force of 1,000 Persians guarding him, the Spartans still managed to surround him and hit him directly on his head with a large stone, killing him instantly. With Mardonius no longer around to lead the Persians to victory, many Persian soldiers began to run back to their camp site but his bodyguards stayed behind to fight on his behalf only to be annihilated by the Greeks. Replacing Mardonius for the remainder of the Battle of Plataea, Artabazus, known for commanding the Sieges of Olynthus and Potidea, led 40,000 remaining Persian soldiers away from the battle grounds toward Thessaly in the hopes of eventually reaching the Hellespont.

While the rest of the Greeks continued fighting against the Persians on the other side of the battlefield, the Athenians came out victorious in a rigorous battle against the Thebans. The Thebans ended up retreating in the battle against the Athenians in the opposite direction of the Persians to avoid further defeat. The Greek alliance, now accompanied by the Athenians, invaded the Persian camp site. Initially the Persian forces fought to protect their wall with vigor, but it was eventually compromised as the Persians drew closer and closer together in the camp, ultimately being murdered by the Greeks. It is estimated that after this annihilation by the Greeks, only 3,000 Persian soldiers remained alive of those who retreated.

According to Herodotus, of the approximately 257,000 Persian soldiers who first appeared on the battlefield, it is estimated that only about 43,000 Persian soldiers were left as the battle came to an end. In comparison, the Greeks as a whole are believed to have only lost about 759 soldiers, which include 600 Megarians and Philasians that were annihilated by the Persians' allies, the Theban cavalry. Furthermore, it has been estimated that only 91 Spartans, 16 Tegeans, and 52 Athenians died in combat considering that these three groups were the main forces fighting on the forefront of the battlefield. In total, it has been estimated that between 1,360 and 10,000 Greek casualties occurred during the Battle of Plataea.

Aftermath

The battles of Plataea and Mycale bear great significance in ancient Greek history as the two battles that put a stop to the second Persian invasion of Greece, causing the Greco-Persian War to lean toward the favor of the Greeks. Furthermore, the Greeks stopped the Persians from invading the rest of Europe as well. The battles also signify the superiority of the hoplite weaponry and armor compared to that of the Persian infantry. Going forward, the Persian infantry began enlisting Greek mercenaries because of their well-made materials in times of battle, demonstrating the vulnerability of the Persian forces.

Chapter 5:
Battle of the 300 Champions

The Battle of the 300 Champions, also known as the Battle of the Champions in the time of Herodotus, was fought long after the Battle of Thermopylae and the Battle of Plataea in 546 B.C. between Argos and Sparta. Instead of enlisting the assistance of entire armed forces for this battle, both sides agreed to only recruit their best, most physically fit warriors with the winner of the battle acquiring new territory. The agreement to recruit an equal number of warriors on each side was presumed to serve the purpose of ensuring a fair fight by reducing the potential for a large amount of casualties. In the end, both armed forces marched to their home fronts to avoid the possibility for escalation of the battle.

According to Herodotus, the Spartans had closed in on and seized the plain of Thyrea. While the Argives moved forward to defend the plain, the two opposing armed forces appeared to be perfectly matched so that neither side would be able to one-up the other. The only way to gain victory in this particular battle was to ensure complete annihilation of the opposing side. In addition, it was also agreed between the Argives and the Spartans that member of their troops who became wounded on the battlefield would not be permitted to be taken by the opposing side. A short-lived battle, both the Argives and the Spartans fought against each other until the sun went down and only three men were left on the battle field, two Argive warriors and one Spartan warrior. The two Argives, whose names were Alcenor and Chromius, were at the time confident that they had killed off all of the men in the Spartan armed forces and they had fled the battle grounds to head back to their homes in Argos to celebrate their victory over the

Spartans with the inhabitants of their city-state. However, much to their surprise, they had made one minor error on the battlefield: Orthryades, a wounded member of the Spartan armed forces, had survived the battle. Essentially the last man standing, Orthryades ran home to Sparta to celebrate his supposed victory as well. Orthryades made it all the way to his baggage handlers to tell them of his news and he committed suicide shortly after. Traditionally, Orthryades was not proud to be the last of his troop to survive the battle and it is believed that he took his own life out of survivor's guilt rather than returning to his home in Sparta. Despite this theory for his suicide being in question by some historians, the actions of Orthyrades is significant to the Battle of the 300 Champions because he did not die at the hands of an Argive soldier.

As a result of this misconception by the Argives and the Spartans, both sides of the battle were able to claim to their home fronts that they came out victorious. The Argives were able to claim their victory because, as they initially agreed with the Spartans prior to the beginning of the battle, they left the battle grounds with more survivors. However, the Spartans were also able to claim their victory because it was a Spartan that remained on the field while the two remaining Argives technically fled before the battle could be considered officially over. In the end, the Spartans were the technical winners of the Battle of the 300 Champions and, as a result, they became the new proud owners of the region Thyreatis.

Chapter 6:
The Fall of the Spartan Empire

The city-state of Sparta, which had command of over 3,500 square miles during its classical period, it was one of the greatest military powers at the time. Years after the Battle of the 300 Champions, from 431 to 404 B.C., the Spartans' Peloponnese League took part in the Battle of Mantinea against the democratic power of the imperial Athens' navy forces. The battle lasted longer than either side had originally expected with the Spartan expecting to come out on top with ease. Six years after the initial start of the Battle of Mantinea, in 425 B.C., the Spartan armed forces decided to fake an attack on the region of Pylos on the southwestern Peloponnese coast line, but the Athenian naval troops surprised the Spartans, surrounding them on the island and remind the Spartans that they were not completely indestructible.

More significant to the fall of the Spartan empire, the Athenians' involvement in Pylos during the Battle of Mantinea also inspired the Spartans' government-owned serfs, the Helots, to ponder the possibility of independence and freedom. The Spartans' now feared the potential for a revolt by the Helots which stemmed from manifestation of the Pylos stronghold while the Athenians feared an imperial collapse of their city-state. Although the Spartans and the Athenians agreed to a sort of peace treaty, the Athenians still did not believe that the Spartans could be trusted and began to question their integrity, taking notice of the Spartans secretive ways. With the Athenians eventually surrendering, the Spartans scored a major victory in the battle.

However, thirty-four years after the Battle of Mantinea ended, Sparta was eliminated from the armed forces of Greece, signifying the decline of Spartan power and political influence. There were two kinds of Helots: natives of Laconia and the Messenian Helots, inhabitants of the westernmost point of the Peloponnese who at one point had been free citizens but were taken over by Spartans during the 7th and 8th centuries B.C. The Messenian Helots had not forgotten their former freedom and often acted stubbornly toward their Spartan masters whenever the opportunity arose. During the Battle of Mantinea, many of these Helots fled to the camp site of the Athenians at Pylos, causing the Spartans a mass panic.

Because Spartan society depended so heavily on the manipulation of the Helots for the sake of fulfilling agricultural and other laborious duties as well as gatekeepers during war times, the Spartans enlisted a group called the Similars to keep a watchful eye on the Helots for any signs of a revolt. In fact, to further remind the Helots of their place in the Sparta society, the Spartans would declare war against the Helots every year and individually humiliate them. The Spartans also enlisted a team of assassins who would murder any Helots who acted rebellious in any way, shape, or form at night. As the Spartans began to find more value in the Helots' services, they began to transition the Helots from being butchered at random to recruiting them as mercenaries in battle. However, this makes more apparent an issue that had risen in seriousness by the end of the 5th century B.C.: the declining population of Similars due to war time casualties forced an even heavier reliance on the Helots by the Spartans. Once the Peloponnesian War broke out, Spartan society was wavering and could no longer successfully shield itself from outlying Greek and Mediterranean influence. Thus, the Spartans were deployed far from their home in Sparta, far enough away from the careful observation of their neighbors, and for extended periods of time. As the society of Sparta strived to meet the Athenians' abilities to enlist mercenaries, maintain spread out armed forces for extended periods of time, and assemble a respectable naval force, the Spartan economy greatly expanded which caused fewer opportunities for Spartans to acquire wealth.

Following the Spartan victory in the Battle of Mantinea in 404 B.C., Sparta made alliances as quickly as they broke them with little concern for the consequences as many well-connected members of Spartan society engaged in irresponsible, greedy, and opportunistic military operations and many Spartans found that their home's government did not acknowledge or address such behavior. Other Greeks, whether friends or foes of the Spartans, were no longer impressed by the Spartans and assembled an anti-Spartan coalition. Rapidly losing their diplomatic credibility, the Spartans had no other choice than to attempt to maintain a respected authority through corrupt tactics demonstrated by their armed forces.

The Battle of Coronea in 394 B.C. was a prime example of this. Spartan hoplites were still without a match; however, approximately 350 men were lost, and, thus, victories for Sparta proved to be too costly. Each casualty on the battlefield equaled one less Similar to fight against Sparta's increasingly numerous and driven internal and external enemies. Furthermore, it was no longer evident that Sparta's complete domination of usual hoplite tactics would continue to hold strong. During 390 B.C., the Spartans were shocked by the loss of an secluded Spartan regiment, and a loss of some 250 soldiers by an Athenian force of soldiers and armed, mobile, and incredibly skilled mercenaries who used spears and shields, customary tactics, and weaponry inspired by the mercenary Thracians from the Black Sea shoreline. Meanwhile, Sparta's rivals were discovering more and more about Sparta's military strategies on the battlefield. It had long been acknowledged wisdom by the Similars that Spartans should avoid fighting the same opponent too frequently. By the time 371 B.C. rolled around, the Thebans had battled the Spartans somewhat continuously for more than two decades and the Theban generals took notice that the Spartans' strengths and weaknesses on the battlefield could be easily exploited to their advantage.

By the Roman era, Sparta had resort to being nothing more than a vacation destination for other Europeans as tourists flocked from around the Greek world to witness Spartan boys suffer through brutal whippings in traditional strength competitions conveniently held in outdoors to accommodate the large crowds of bystanders. These disturbing sources of tourist entertainment stood as unfortunate reminders of the dedication to punishment and public duty that had maintained a formerly proud society of Similar soldiers. Today, the Greek city-state of Sparta is a lively location in the center of Greece with the Eurotas valley in beautiful condition. However, there is little archaeological evidence of the valley's celebrated yet dreadful history. And ironically, the ruins of Messene, where the Helots previously resided, which stand high atop the Kalamata plain, have remained far more remarkable.

Conclusion

Thank you again for downloading this book!

I hope this book was able to help you to gain a deeper understanding of the rise and fall of Spartan society.

The next step is to attempt to relate this knowledge to modern day society.

Finally, if you enjoyed this book, then I'd like to ask you for a favor, would you be kind enough to leave a review for this book on Amazon? It'd be greatly appreciated!

Thank you and good luck!

Bibliography

Diodorus Siculus. *Diodorus of Sicily in Twelve Volumes,* trans. C. H. Oldfather, Vol 4-8, Cambridge, Mass.: Harvard University Press; London: William Heinemann Ltd., 1989

Forrest, W.G. *A History of Sparta, 950-192 B.C.,* New York: W. W. Norton & Company, 1968

Hanson, Victor Davis. *The Western Way of War: Infantry Battle in Classical Greece,* Berkeley, Los Angeles, and London: University of California Press 1989

Herodotus. *The History,* trans. George Rawlinson, New York: D. Appleman and Company, 1885 4:7

Niebuhr Tod, Marcus. "Sparta" *The Encyclopædia Britannica: A Dictionary of Arts, Sciences, Literature and General Information,* Encyclopædia Britannica Inc., London 1911, 11:611

Plutarch. "Apophthegmata Laconica" *Moralia,* trans. Frank Cole Babbit, ed. *Moralia* Vol. III, Loeb Classical Library, Cambridge: Harvard University Press, 2004

Tyrtæus, Theocritus, Bion, Moschus. *The Idylls of Theocritus, Bion, and Moschus, and the War Songs of Tyrtæus,* trans. The Rev. J. Banks, M.A., London: George Bell and Sons 1878

Wikipedia

"4th Century BC," *History of Sparta* 5 Mar. 2016. Web. 6 Mar. 2016 https://en.wikipedia.org/wiki/History_of_Sparta #cite_ref-97

"Hellenistic and Roman Sparta," *Sparta* 29 Feb. 2016. Web.   6   Mar. 2016 https://en.wikipedia.org/wiki/Sparta

300. Dir. Zack Snyder. Warner Bros., Legendary Pictures, Virtual Studios, Hollywood Gang Productions, Atmosphere Entertainment MM, Mel's Cite du Cinema, Nimar Studios 2006

Trojan Horse:
How The Greeks Won The Trojan War'

Introduction

The Trojan War was an epic battle that ended when the Trojan Horse filled with Greeks was received inside the city gates of Troy. This is the summation of what could be history or myth.

According to Homer's Iliad and The Odyssey, the Trojan War was fought because of gods and goddesses, who always liked to play with humans. History tells of something much different. In fact, for several centuries, historians have been trying to prove that Troy actually existed and was not a mythical city.

Until 1871, it was believed the Trojan War was nothing but an epic poem, created by a Greek poet, Homer. It was considered a fictitious account, with no bearing on the real world whatsoever.

Few facts were known prior to 1871, which could be used to determine there was ever such a battle between Greek forces and Trojans protecting their coastal city. It wasn't that war didn't exist or that the Trojans weren't real. It was rather the sparse historical accounts of such an epic war. Plenty of poems and stories based on mythical gods and goddesses were written years after the supposed war, but nothing in the actual history books of the time or since the "Trojan War" lent to the credibility of the story.

Yet, the legend created by Homer continued to plague historians and archeologists. It became a mission for some individuals, including Heinrich Schliemann and Frank Calvert to prove Troy was an actual city that existed in times of antiquity.

Today the question is not about whether Troy existed or did not. It is now fact that there was a city called Troy, where the Trojans lived, and it was under continued battle against enemy forces.

The real question is—did the Trojan War, as we have come to think of it happen or was it a series of small battles that eventually led to the end of the Trojan people?

Was there, in fact, a Trojan Horse and if so, how did it help win the war for the Greeks?

The focus of the coming chapters, will be to discuss the Trojan Horse as a real concept, not the fictional one from Homer's epic poem. The focus will not be to tell you how Achilles entered the city and helped win the war.

Instead, you will learn who the Trojans were, which Greek faction fought against the Trojans in the last battle, and why the war or series of wars occurred, which led to the innovative concept of the Trojan Horse. In the end, you will also learn the impact the "Trojan Horse" has had on more recent wars. You will discover if the Trojans died out never to be heard of again or if one war ended and more simply occurred.

Chapter 1:
The Bronze Age

Background is needed to answer why the Trojan War occurred and how the Trojan horse was used to win the war. By becoming familiar with the Bronze Age, you can begin to understand the puzzle archeologists are finally starting to uncover.

The Bronze Age is defined by the smelting of copper and tin or by the trading of bronze products. It is also categorized as the third millennium B.C. However, this means different things depending on the regions of the world being discussed.

The Near East, which categorizes the following countries: Anatolia, Elam, Caucasus, Egypt, Mesopotamia, the Levant, and Sistan, were in the Bronze Age from 3300 to 1200 B.C. Later, you should remember that Anatolia was also considered Asia Minor. Anatolia is now called Turkey.

South Asia was said to be in the Bronze Age from 3000 to 1200 B.C. Europe, which includes Aegean began their Bronze Age in 3200 to 600 B.C. Greece was considered as a part of Europe even then, and had a hold on Aegean property, as well as control of the Aegean Sea.

To put these Bronze Age dates into perspective, Greece was a mighty power starting from 1600 B.C. to the end of 1100 B.C.

Note: Many historians trying to prove the existence of Troy, the Trojan War, and the Trojan Horse, believe the Bronze Age ended in 1100 B.C. in Greece and much of the Near East. This will not be debated in this book.

According to the Troia Archeological Site website and UNESCO World Heritage Site, the land considered to be a part of the City of Troy was inhabited from 3000 B.C. to 500 A.D.

The part of this wide range in time period that most concerns us is 1300 to 1000 B.C. It is generally accepted that Homer's Troy and the Troy that fell due to the Greek's Trojan Horse existed sometime between 1300 and 1150 B.C.

Carl Blegen was an archeologist, who worked on the site now considered Troy, between 1932 and 1938. Blegen's chronology of the Troy Strata provides a look at 1300 to 1000 B.C.

Strata is a geological term meaning the layers of earth archeologists have dug up in an attempt to discover historical evidence that will help us understand the ancient civilizations of Troy.

These strata are named by site level: Troy VIh, Troy VIIa, Troy VIIb1, Troy VIIb2, and Troy VIIb3. There is an approximate end date for each site level, meaning the civilization that existed prior to the dates was in some way damaged.

Troy VIh was said to have ended in 1300 B.C. due to an earthquake. Any buildings, people, and artifacts discovered from this time period show a great geological event, such as an earthquake that made people flee and leave everyday items behind.

The next end date for Troy, was 1230-1190/1180 BC, which was Troy VIIa. The listed probably cause was an attack by an enemy. In 1150 BC, Troy VIIb1 was destroyed by an unknown cause. Troy VIIb2 ended in 1100 BC, either due to an earthquake or enemy attack. Troy VIIb3 ended sometime in 1000 BC from an unknown cause.

Troy VIIa is the most important strata. Several archeologists, including Blegen, Schliemann, Calvert, and Strauss accept that the Troy mentioned in the Iliad and Odyssey; therefore, the Troy associated with the war was the Troy VIIa. Blegen has more to support the claim. When digging to the Troy VIIa, he uncovered many unburied skeletons, with Mycenaean Greek arrowheads near the bodies, suggesting the war occurred.

As the discussion deepens about Troy, the Mycenaean Greeks, and the Trojan Horse, remember the probable "Trojan War" was sometime around 1230 to 1180 B.C. This has to do with the unburied skeletons, carbon dating of those skeletons, and the geological evidence that provides a narrowed timeline. The main evidence to suggest this is when the 10 years of war occurred, is a lack of any other cause for the destruction of the city, as well as Homer's account. It also sets a timeline for the information to come in discussing why the war started and how it ended.

Chapter 2:
Who Were the Trojans

Archeologists and historians generally accept that Trojans are a mixture of Anatolian and Luwian origins. This was not always the case. For years, the only evidentiary support that Troy and Trojans existed was Homer's tales. It might seem like the book keeps bringing in Homer and the question of the history versus the myth, but in actuality, to understand the full answer this book is going to provide, you must have a knowledge of the "players."

In Homer's account of the epic war, he used the Greek spelling for names. It seems obvious now that he did so because he was Greek and because when the story was written Greek was a well-known language. To earlier archeologists who were trying to prove the City of Troy existed, there was a 10-year war, and the Greeks won, any information from Homer's epic poems that corresponded to known history was important.

Archeological digs have since answered the question of who the Trojans really were, without any mythological or inaccurate historical assumptions. Archeologists firmly believe the Trojan people were of Anatolian and Luwian decent because of artifacts, buildings, and rituals.

Historical Context Uncovered by Schliemann and Others

Frank Calvert went to what is now Turkey to uncover the true City of Troy. He was not a very well-known archeologist at the time, mostly due to lack of funding and being self-taught. Heinrich Schliemann was largely considered a fraud and discounted for his belief in Troy, but he at least had the funds to make the dig known to the world and to tell the newspapers that he had at last found the real Troy. This occurred in 1871.

What Schliemann considered Troy was little more than a mound of earth, some uncovered bits of pottery, and a deep belief that he was right. Like many in the archeologic and the scientific academia world, proving or discounting a theory is powerful stuff.

Archeologists like Blegen, who arrived in Turkey in 1932, came with the idea of proving Troy existed and uncovered half an acre of the city. It was the citadel. Fast-forward 130 years since Schliemann found his mound, and it is 1988. Strauss and others did their part to uncover a total of 75 acres of city.

In the 1930s, historians postulated that Troy was a mere citadel on the coast of Turkey and not the opulent fortress that the Greeks feared. Yet, 50 years later, with more digging, more strata uncovered, and reaching Troy VIIa, it was known that the city was every bit as large as Homer depicted in his epic tale. It is also at this time, origins of who the Troy descended from were uncovered.

The City Layout, Pottery, and Burials

With the entire city of Troy uncovered by archeologists, work could begin uncovering the Trojans' origins. The city layout represented Anatolian construction. The position of the citadel versus other buildings, including the architecture of those buildings represented the Anatolian culture more so than the Mycenaean Greek culture.

Quite a bit of pottery was uncovered. Again, the majority of the pieces represented an Anatolian connection, where the minority of pieces related more to Greece. Given the shipping lanes for goods coming from Asia through the Aegean Sea and past the strait, where Troy was built, it is not unlikely that traders from Greece sold their pottery in Troy.

Archeological digs uncovered burial grounds, which indicated Anatolian burial practices versus those of the Greeks.

If you add in the location of the city, which was in Anatolia or what is now called Turkey, it would make sense for the Trojans to be descendants of earlier Anatolian people.

There is evidence to suggest a larger Greek population did live in Troy, but this was after the Trojan War is thought to have occurred. This evidence is based on layers of artifacts, in which Greek artifacts were found in strata nearer to the top than Trojan relics.

Where Science Has Yet to Reach

DNA mapping is now possible. More and more species, including human species are being mapped to determine origins. Quite a bit about the skeletons found from prehistoric eras is known thanks to DNA. However, the skeletons found at Troy and thought to have been involved in the Trojan War have yet to undergo DNA profiling, at least that has been released to the public for consumption.

When assessing information for DNA confirmation, it seems scientists have made it as far back as determining the origins of the Etruscans. This is mentioned only to show that the Trojan heritage did not die out completely. DNA evidence shows Etruscan origins relate to the Hittite, and Lydian Kingdoms. Troy was a part of these two kingdoms. More detail about the Hittites will be discussed in chapters about why the Trojan War occurred.

Given the interest in Troy in the academic world, it is likely that DNA profiling of skeletons found at the City of Troy will someday be conducted as a way to answer more questions about the time and the people who lived there.

For now, the simplest answer to who were the Trojans is— Anatolian descendants.

Chapter 3:
The Mycenaean Greeks

In any war there are always at least two parties involved, if not a few other countries because they share alliances with one of the main parties waging war. It might seem a waste of words to discuss who the Greeks were. When discussing the Trojans, there is a question because early assumptions said they were descendants of Greece, when in fact the Trojans displayed more of an Anatolian heritage.

You might even say, "duh they were Greeks." But did you know, there were Mycenaean Greeks and Dorian Greeks living during the Bronze Age? Were you aware that certain cities like Pylos and Athens were populated by Mycenaean Greeks and many of the Dorian Greeks had started to migrate out of Greece, weakening their strong positions as they headed across Europe?

As with many cultures, there are clear divisions, even within a broad term to mean a certain origin. A great example shows that today, labelling someone from Korea as Asian. Yes, Asia as a continent is very large, but it encompasses many cultures, who are diverse in their beliefs, way of life, and language. Chinese is very distinctive from Korean, as is Japanese from the other two languages. Therefore, it is important to know who the Mycenaean Greeks were.

The Mycenaean Period

The Mycenaean period is a time when the Greek mainland was enjoying power and wealth. Their strong holds were Mycenae, Thebes, Tiryns, and Athens. Greek workshops were filled with pottery, bronze, jewelry, carved gems, vases, glass ornaments, and precious metals.

The Mycenaean Greeks had a wide reach for their commerce, sending goods from Greece through the Mediterranean, basically extending from Spain to the Levant. Evidence from this time suggests vases, oil, and wine were the primary goods of trade.

These Greeks were more than traders. They were also warriors and engineers. They created bridges, beehive-shaped tombs, and fortification walls using Cyclopean masonry. The Mycenaean's also established irrigation and drainage systems. Mycenae was viewed as a rich city of gold, while Pylos was sandy (Homer's description). Tablet evidence that were used to record history by scribes, indicated Greece had a very organized feudal system in place. According to Colette Hemingway and Sean Hemingway, the late 1300 century B.C. or 1200s, was a time of decline for the Mycenaean Greeks. The important sites, which had been filled with wealth, suffered destruction, and many Mycenaean's started moving to remote settlements. Pylos, which was the city the king inhabited was destroyed sometime in 1200 B.C. However, it is not completely gone, since it is still a city in Greece and called Pylos-Nestoras today.

Historians consider the complete collapse of the Mycenaean Greeks occurred by the end of 1100 B.C., while many collapses in their cities from 1300 to 1180 B.C. threatened ultimate destruction. It was also a time of rebuilds for parts of the cities the Greeks felt were important.

There is a bit of debate about this time, where some scholars feel it was the population movement that made the Mycenaean's weak. Those who study the Trojan War are more inclined to think it was internal battles, as well as trying to over-stretch their forces to expand and take over cities of shipping importance.

Other Important Players

The world did not consist of just the Trojans and Mycenaean Greeks. There was a lot of strife, natural disasters, and internal wars that started to change existing kingdoms beyond what occurred in Troy and Mycenaean Greek cities.

The Hittites ran a powerful kingdom, which also included Troy. Around the same time Troy fell, Hattusa, the capital of the Hittite Kingdom, was destroyed. Aramaic nomads and Chaldeans were threatening the survival of the Assyrian and Babylonian empires. The Dorian Greeks were migrating and expanding, causing trouble for the Mycenaean Greeks.

It was suggested that the Mycenaean's and Hittites had a peaceful relationship, due to respect and mutual fear of destruction. An accord between Hittite King Hattusili III and King Ahhiyawa of the Mycenaean Greeks existed.

However, Egyptian factions and others like Piyama-Radu constantly moved against the Hittite Kingdom. These two cultures wanted to expand from Africa into Asia, and this was difficult because the Hittite fortress walls were strong. King Ahhiyawa was given Lesbos by Piyama-Radu during the 13th Century B.C. Piyama-Radu even tried to enter Troy as a way to get to the capital of the Hittite Kingdom.

Evidence suggests the relationship with Piyama-Radu was more important to the Greeks than keeping the peace with the Hittite King. Although, for a time after King Hattusili III asked to restore peace, King Ahhiyawa did accept.

Click here to check out the rest of Trojan Horse on Amazon.com

Or go to: **http://www.amazon.co.uk/dp/B01CKJOR0C**
(If in the UK)

Made in the USA
San Bernardino, CA
23 June 2016